Dear Parent:
Your child's love of reading starts here!

Every child learns to read in a different way and at his or her own speed. Some go back and forth between reading levels and read favorite books again and again. Others read through each level in order. You can help your young reader improve and become more confident by encouraging his or her own interests and abilities. From books your child reads with you to the first books he or she reads alone, there are I Can Read Books for every stage of reading:

SHARED READING
Basic language, word repetition, and whimsical illustrations, ideal for sharing with your emergent reader

BEGINNING READING
Short sentences, familiar words, and simple concepts for children eager to read on their own

READING WITH HELP
Engaging stories, longer sentences, and language play for developing readers

READING ALONE
Complex plots, challenging vocabulary, and high-interest topics for the independent reader

ADVANCED READING
Short paragraphs, chapters, and exciting themes for the perfect bridge to chapter books

I Can Read Books have introduced children to the joy of reading since 1957. Featuring award-winning authors and illustrators and a fabulous cast of beloved characters, I Can Read Books set the standard for beginning readers.

A lifetime of discovery begins with the magical words "I Can Read!"

Visit www.icanread.com for information
on enriching your child's reading experience.

To Mark, Sam, and the Little One

ISBN 978-1-338-60078-0

Copyright © 2016 by Sam Garton. All rights reserved. Published by Scholastic Inc., 557 Broadway, New York, NY 10012, by arrangement with HarperCollins Children's Books, a division of HarperCollins Publishers. I Can Read Book® is a trademark of HarperCollins Publishers. SCHOLASTIC and associated logos are trademarks and/or registered trademarks of Scholastic Inc.

The publisher does not have any control over and does not assume any responsibility for author or third-party websites or their content.

12 11 10 9 8 7 6 5 4 3 2   19 20 21 22 23 24

Printed in the U.S.A.   40

First Scholastic printing, September 2019

OTTER
Hello, Sea Friends!

By SAM GARTON

SCHOLASTIC INC.

Otter Keeper is taking me
on a trip!
Teddy is coming too.

We are going to meet animals
that live in the sea.

We buy tickets.

Teddy doesn't need one.

This place is big.

Otter Keeper has a map.

I don't need a map.

First we find lots of fish.

They are pretty.

We try to count them,

but there are too many.

We find some seals.

They are playing a game!

The seals have lots of fun.

I wish I could play too.

We find a big turtle.

He swims very slowly.

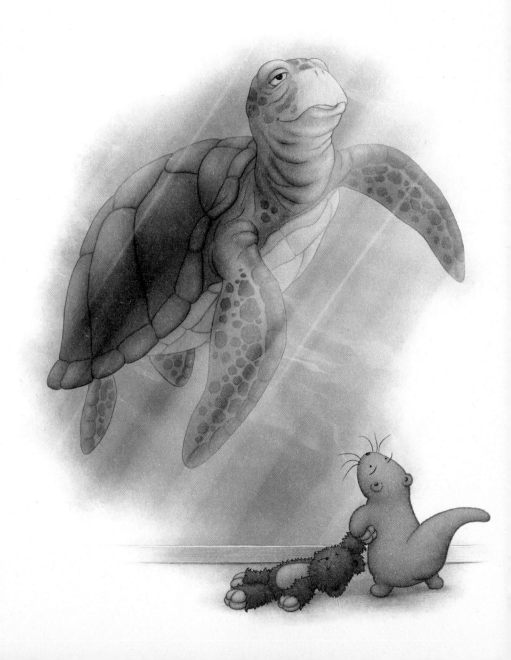

He comes to say hello.

I like the turtle.

We even meet a shark.

He is a bit scary!

I stay close to Otter Keeper
just in case.

It is time for lunch.

I share mine with Teddy.

Then we go to the play area.

It is not for the animals.

It is for me.

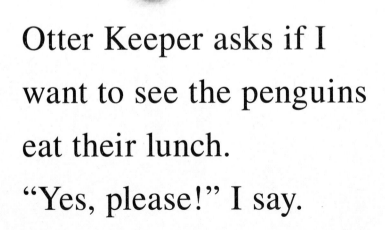

Otter Keeper asks if I
want to see the penguins
eat their lunch.
"Yes, please!" I say.

Yuck! The penguins
are eating smelly fish!

We have met lots of
animals, but penguins are
the best.

Oh no! Teddy!

The nice man saves Teddy.

"Teddy wanted to make
friends," I say.

We all tell Teddy to be
more careful.

It is time to go home.

I do not want to go.

Otter Keeper says we can
visit the gift shop first.

There are lots of things
to buy!

But Teddy and I
know what we want.

Now we have a new friend!